# WIN WIN WORKBOOK

## STAY ON TARGET TO MITIGATE LEGAL RISK FOR THE COMMON GOOD

### REBECCA SPOSITA, ESQ.

HIGHERLIFE
PUBLISHING & MARKETING

HigherLife Development Services, Inc.,

PO Box 623307, Oviedo, FL 32762

(407) 563-4806, higherlifepublishing.com

Edited by Esse Johnson

Published 2024

Printed in the United States of America

30 29 28 27 26 25 24 1 2 3 4 5

ISBN: 978-1-964081-99-1 (paperback)

ISBN: 978-1-964081-32-8 (eBook)

Library of Congress record: 1-14302286591

# CONTENTS

# INTRODUCTION

When I wrote my book, *WIN WIN: Helping Organizations Mitigate Legal Risk for the Common Good,* my intention was to spark a shift in the way executives approach organizational complaints, with an aim to minimize litigation and re-traumatization. What caught me off guard, however, was the overwhelming interest from various levels within the organizations. Executives sought systemic approaches, while others foresaw the challenge of turning theory into practice in the heat of a moment. Many asked how they could teach these principles effectively to their teams.

I crafted this workbook as a practical guide so you can do just that. Its purpose is to equip administrators, managers, supervisors, HR representatives, risk management officers, and legal counsel to handle complaints with empathy and efficiency. By following the straightforward techniques outlined here, you'll learn how to navigate complaints in a manner that alleviates stress, validates concerns, and mitigates the risk of escalation.

Each chapter is focused on an important characteristic of an effective response. These characteristics are to be integrated through every stage of the reporting process. In *WIN WIN*, I detailed these differing stages and gave real-life examples of complaints that either spiraled from the walls of the organization to the steps of the courthouse, or were nipped in the bud and constructively resolved. I also discussed the psychology of trauma and how a claimant can be triggered or made more anxious by a non-trauma-informed reporting process, negatively impacting your team's outcomes. Here I build on that foundation by presenting the material in an easy-to-teach format that you can quickly review and present, along with common questions and answers. And while it isn't necessary to read *WIN WIN* prior to using this workbook, I do recommend it to better understand the complexity of trauma, and how people can easily become overwhelmed by the organizational maze of filing a complaint or raising a concern that requires an organizational response.

I've termed my approach an On-TARGET Response. On the one hand, our "target" focus is to avoid litigation, a goal that every organization aims to achieve when faced with a potential lawsuit. On the other hand, and personally, my primary "target" is to see claimants treated with greater respect and understanding. While I am a plaintiff litigation attorney and make my living pursuing claims against organizations and institutions, I am first and foremost a client advocate. I want my clients treated better when they first raise their concerns, even if it means they ultimately don't file a lawsuit. While I'm confident I'll never run out of business, I'm equally confident that you can do better business by humanely and effectively addressing problems before they get ugly. I can't tell you how often clients come to me with a lawsuit that could have been prevented had the issue been addressed immediately, or if the client had been treated fairly and their needs addressed. Even if an immediate and right response costs some money, in the long run it can save you much more than it cost—because as you well know, the longer the conflict continues the more money and resources it costs the organization.

Not all problems can escape litigation, but there's another reason to implement an On-TARGET Response and that's to minimize your own stress. No matter what the conflict is, who the parties are, or whether or not it ends up in court, no one likes a problem. The man or woman coming to you with the problem surely doesn't want to be there. You already have plenty of work to do. A new issue will add to your workload. It will draw you into all the messy politics of the organization as you seek to please everyone who needs pleasing. Every encounter with the parties involved will be an emotional and potentially explosive one. The constant stress may lead you to say things you wish you'd never said (or fail to say things you wish you had). You may project your irritation and frustration onto other people who have nothing to do with it. And the investigation may shine a light on emails and other communications you'd rather not have to disclose. Avoiding all of this begins with an On-TARGET Response. An On-TARGET Response in your organizational reporting process will minimize that stress, reduce your workload, make it less likely that the issue drags on for months or years, and reduce the potential that your communications get subpoenaed.

---

# ELEMENTS OF AN
# On-TARGET RESPONSE

## Trauma-Informed
## Accountable
## Respectful and Responsive
## Genuine
## Empowering
## Transparent

---

I've developed the On-TARGET acronym to help you remember the basic principles of an effective response to someone who has been injured or harmed. An On-TARGET Response increases the chances of an early resolution and helps to prevent future incidences because it is Trauma-Informed, Accountable, Respectful and Responsive, Genuine, Empowering, and Transparent.

## TRAUMA-INFORMED

Let's start with Trauma-Informed. Trauma can change the way people process information and how they communicate. It can shut down or amplify emotional reactions, which in turn may alter how you perceive their credibility. This concept is adapted from new directives in social and health services that call for trauma-informed care. It doesn't mean you have to pamper everyone who makes a complaint, believe everything happened just the way they said it did, or take the side of anyone who says they've suffered an injustice. It means *beginning with an understanding of how trauma impacts people.*

Offering a trauma-informed response also means making subtle but meaningful shifts in how a complaint is processed. These nuanced shifts can significantly change how someone feels they've been treated. When people feel they've been heard and treated fairly, they are far less likely to take further action, go public, or see an attorney. They are often satisfied just to be heard, their suffering acknowledged, the problem corrected, and to be compensated for any direct damages they've suffered. But when they feel that reporting what happened to them has made them less safe or more harmed, let me tell you, that's when things can get ugly.

That's when the widow whose husband died in an accident rejects every settlement offer because she's determined to restore her husband's reputation at trial. That's when the parents of a newborn injured from oxygen deprivation now requiring around-the-clock assistance for life will not be satisfied with any amount of money, and will want to strip the physician of the right to practice while taking punitive measures against the hospital. And that's when the sexual assault victim will make sure her story is told in the international press, taking down everyone who disbelieved her up and down the pipeline. People who seek early remedies to legitimate wrongs but find themselves being treated and perceived as the problem will demand and need more to make them whole again—because the process itself has damaged them.

Because nothing can undo the traumatizing effect of trying to report a wrongdoing and being treated badly, <u>those who have been abused by the process itself are the ones who won't go away quietly.</u>

## ACCOUNTABLE

Being accountable is not the same as accepting liability. I understand that when someone comes to you with their concerns or a negative report, you're accountable to determine the facts and protect your organization. But you're also accountable to your stakeholders—employees, customers, and anyone who may potentially be harmed on your property or by your agents. You're accountable for fairly and effectively gathering the evidence, listening to the parties involved, and taking whatever steps you can to address the problem. And, as far as the scope of your position will allow, you're accountable for righting any wrong that could put your organization or any of its stakeholders at risk. Taking care of hazards or potential hazards is not admitting liability. It's being accountable.

## RESPECTFUL AND RESPONSIVE

Most people think they treat others with respect. And most people believe that in their professional capacity, they are responsive to others when someone comes to them with a problem or concern. But the reality is that one of the first instincts people have when the bearer of bad news appears is to stop the bad news in its tracks. And they often do that not by addressing the problem, but by shooting the messenger. They deny the problem and cast the one who brought it to their attention as unreliable (at best) or a mentally unstable liar (at worst). As I point out throughout this workbook, this does not make the problem go away. It more often makes it bigger—and costlier. Instead, by being respectful at every level of the organizational process and responding constructively to the problem, you are more likely to resolve the issue, protect your organization's reputation, and avoid a lawsuit.

## GENUINE

What do I mean by genuine? I mean, don't just say you are respectful. Don't just say you are responsive to the problem.

And don't just say you're doing all you can. Be genuine. Treat the person who comes to you with a concern or injury as you would your supervisor, your spouse, or your child. Treat them as you would want to be treated. Be honest. Be real. People can smell a false promise, a platitude, or an outright lie, and when they do, they won't trust anything you say or do from that point on. If they do believe falsities, when they learn otherwise—and they will—they will feel betrayed. Betrayal sparks a primal reaction. They will become angry and determined to seek justice. To avoid that outcome, be genuine from the start.

## EMPOWERING

One of the principles of trauma-informed care is that someone experiencing trauma needs to be given as much control as possible over the situation. We never have absolute control over anything in our lives, but when someone has experienced a traumatic injury or loss, they are all the more devastated because they don't feel they have any control over their lives or what has happened to them. By empowering someone who has been harmed by or at your organization, you can minimize their distress—and thus, your own stress. How do you do that? You clarify their choices. What are their options? What steps can they take to protect themselves? If you emphasize the many ways they can make decisions throughout the process, they will leave your office feeling better. If they leave your office feeling like everything is in someone else's hands, they will feel diminished and seek power through other means.

## TRANSPARENT

Finally, it's important in any On-TARGET Response that you are as transparent as possible throughout the process. Secret meetings and proceedings, withholding documents, or other means of keeping someone "out of the loop" or denying them information they have a right to does two things: it increases the chance of litigation so they can use the discovery process to obtain the information, and it increases the likelihood that they will go to the media where the freedom of the press will prevail. To avoid this outcome, be transparent right from the start and at every level of the process.

Now that you have a basic understanding of what an On-TARGET Response entails, let's take a closer look at what each of these dimensions means in an organizational setting and how you can put them into practice.

———

## I. REVIEW QUESTIONS

In my experience presenting this material, executives sought _____ approaches, while others foresaw the challenge of

_____

_____.

Describe the overly common and erroneous approach in response to a claimant that often escalates the situation, almost ensuring a costly lawsuit.

What is the acronym for an empathic and effective response that mitigates risk of a lawsuit and helps to avoid re-traumatization of the claimant?

What do the letters of the acronym stand for?

**ADDITIONAL NOTES:**

# CHAPTER 1
## TRAUMA-INFORMED

"Get over it," "It's not that bad," and "Just move on," are common responses to a problem someone brings to the attention of an organization. You might think it's no big deal, but the problem might indeed be a big deal. It could be such a big deal that you're uncomfortable even having to sit in the same room with the parents whose baby or child has just died, the woman whose rape kit clarifies that she was indeed sexually assaulted, or the man who will never walk again. Now they're blaming your organization, and they want you to do something. But you don't work for them. You work for the organization. Yet here they are acting as if you're the one to blame. They're angry, furious even. Otherwise, they *should* be, but instead they're talking about the whole thing as if they're reciting a recipe.

"Clearly," it is easy to surmise, "they weren't injured."

Or now they're telling yet another version, adding new details, changing the order of events, or just acting downright crazy. They're not reliable narrators so, we conclude, they're clearly lying. They're making a big deal out of nothing. They're not upset enough. It's not how people who've been injured usually act.

But here's the thing: when someone is traumatized, they don't act rationally. Their brains stop functioning normally and they get stuck in fight-flight-or-freeze mode. That means they may not be thinking clearly. They may forget or block out important details they will remember later. They may shut down. Understand two things:

1.  Whatever it is that happened to them, if they were traumatized, their brains were changed by the event.
2.  People who were traumatized in the past may respond based on how their brains were altered during those previous traumatic experiences.

Now let's consider each of these points in more detail.

## THE EFFECTS OF TRAUMA ON THE BRAIN

The amygdala is a part of the brain that stores memories and processes emotions. The hypothalamus is the part of the brain that regulates the cells, hormones, and organs. When we feel threatened, the amygdala sends a signal to the hypothalamus to ready the body for fight, flight, or freeze. The goal is to survive, and to do that, the body must reserve its energy by shutting down all unnecessary expenditures. In *WIN WIN*, I go into more detail about how the brain is changed by trauma. The important thing to keep in mind is that when we are frightened or shocked, or experience, witness, or suffer something that shakes us from our sense of security and threatens our psychological or physical survival, we enter fight-flight-or-freeze mode.

# FOR FIGHT, FLIGHT, OR FREEZE

- The brain signals the adrenal glands to flood the body with adrenaline.

- The liver produces extra glucose for energy.

- Breathing and heart rate accelerate to ready the body for flight.

- Digestion slows to reserve energy.

- Saliva is no longer produced.

- Blood vessels constrict.

- Vision and hearing block out peripheral details.

When a threat has passed, the body usually returns to its normal state, but for someone who has been repeatedly traumatized such as in childhood abuse, living in a war zone, or any situation that repeatedly puts a person in that state of fight, flight, or freeze, the brain can get stuck in that state. When something happens to reignite it, the process is even more automatic. That's why a person can be triggered by something that seems to you completely unthreatening. But that doesn't mean their trauma isn't your concern. You may be familiar with the legal doctrine of the "eggshell skull." The rule holds that if a person has a cranium as thin as an eggshell and it is shattered by the defendant's actions—even if the action would not have caused a similar injury in someone else—the defendant is liable for the damages the defendant suffered. The takeaway? "It's no big deal" won't cut it. <u>If someone has suffered significantly, and</u>

their suffering is heightened because the event triggered pain from a past trauma, some might shrug it off but you MUST take their suffering seriously.

A similar reaction may happen with someone who has faced an extreme trauma. Even if they have not suffered from repeated or prolonged trauma in their past, if the traumatic injury was extreme or significantly altered their life, their brains could be stuck in that fight-flight-or-freeze mode.

This means that just telling you what happened could cause them to relive the event and revive the traumatized state where the hypothalamus might:

- trigger emotional flooding making them appear wild, crazy, or, conversely,
- shut off all emotion, making them appear unaffected;
- scramble cognitive abilities; or
- block out overly disturbing memories.

Think about driving home in an emotional state. Have you ever pulled into your driveway and wondered how you got there? Maybe you were flooded with the warm emotions of love, or you had to rush home in response to awful news, or you were so angry with your boss that your blood was boiling. When stressed, excited, or in any heightened emotional state, peripheral details will shut down. You may recall bits and pieces in the hours that follow, or you may not. That may be happening to the person sitting across from you in your office retelling a disturbing event, and that's why a lot of what we think we understand about the reliability of witnesses might be mistaken.

## MYTHS ABOUT RELIABILITY OF WITNESSES

*The myth: When claimants "recall" new details in subsequent interviews or when interviewed by other people, they are probably lying.*

**The reality:** Most traumatized people have blocked out important details and some of these details may be remembered over time.

*The myth: If they mix up the sequence of events or change the times or time frame, they are making it up.*

**The reality:** We lose our sense of time when we are traumatized. Our memories are impaired, and we may confuse the order of events.

*The myth: Someone who exhibits no emotion about something that would disturb others is either lying or they weren't that affected by the event.*

**The reality:** Humans sometimes cope with adversity by dissociating, i.e., shutting down emotions in order to distance ourselves from the events. We may then relay information matter-of-factly but internalize and express the trauma in other ways such as self-medicating, self-harm, or delayed emotional breakdown.

*The myth: If someone is babbling endlessly, not focusing on the questions, or shifting from anger to laughter to crying while narrating the event, they are probably mentally unstable and they have bigger problems than the complaint they've brought to you.*

**The reality:** They may be emotionally flooding. Their hypothalamus has kicked into overdrive and their neural pathways are racing from one thought to the next. This is a common response to trauma.

## TAKEAWAYS

- Don't judge the veracity of a complaint based on *how* it is presented. If the event was traumatizing, there is no standard way people will respond or present the information to you.
- Resist the urge to scold, be stern, tell them they are wrong or lying, or otherwise display any aggression because it could intensify their traumatic response.
- Don't judge whether *you* would be traumatized by the event or injury. Listen to how *they* have been affected by it.
- Don't assume that if they act as if it's no big deal, that it's no big deal. They may be suppressing their emotions or they may be struggling to cooperate and appear professional.
- Do everything in your power to help them feel safe talking to you. Listen. Don't interrupt. Take them seriously. Provide them with resources. Show them you understand they've been hurt. Don't become defensive. Ask them what you can do to help.

## FAQS

Q. *It's not my job to provide therapy. Why should their trauma be my responsibility?*

A. Of course it's not your job to provide therapy, nor should you attempt to do so. Your responsibility is to ascertain the facts. Misinterpreting the person's behaviors can cause you to misinterpret the information and draw a costly and wrong conclusion. Understanding the effects of trauma on thinking and behavior protects both you and your organization from avoidable mistakes. You'll have a better understanding of why someone might appear confused, unreliable, or unstable, which will help you get at the truth more quickly and with less stress.

**Q.** *Some of these people are too sensitive. They overreact to everything and then claim to be "traumatized" by the slightest thing. Why should I treat them like fragile dolls?*

A. You shouldn't treat anyone like a fragile doll. You should treat them humanely and kindly. Listen to what they are telling you and how they are feeling. Take them at their word that they are upset. It's quite possible that what seems like a "slight thing" to you has brought back trauma from past abuses. Their complaint about a person or group could also be a red flag to you—take heed before their "slights" escalate into a greater problem. Set your preconceptions, politics, and personal views aside and recognize that something has happened to hurt the person coming to you with a problem. Find out what that is.

**Q.** *Why should we treat people differently just because they've been traumatized in the past?*

A. If you're leading a long hike and one person gets wounded with a broken leg while the others are able-bodied, would you treat the wounded with the same expectation as the others or would you offer more support to the one with the injury? You treat both with kindness and compassion, but one needs more. Treat all people with the same respect, but understand that the incident someone is presenting to you may be traumatic to them. If they have a past history of trauma, they may be even more wounded and may present in ways that appear "off" such as overly emotional, lacking emotion, or confused. An appropriate, trauma-informed response will help *you* avoid costly errors.

**Q.** *How do I know if they've been traumatized by the incident or in the past? Am I supposed to ask them if they've ever been abused?*

A. Don't ask about past abuse unless they bring it up. Your job is to find out what happened. <u>Do</u> ask how they are feeling and if they need resources for support. Many events that traumatize people are not perceived as traumatic, so they may not articulate it in those words. They might even deny something was traumatizing (especially men or anyone who fears appearing weak). But they could be suffering with PTSD, impairing cognition and heightening or confusing emotional responses. The safer the person feels with you, the more likely the effects of trauma will subside.

**Q.** *Why should I tell every man in our office that he can't even pat a woman on the back for a good job because it might "trigger" her? When does it stop?*

A. It stops when everyone is treated humanely and kindly. While a "pat on the back" might seem like no big deal, consider two things. First, if someone comes to you reporting an unwelcome "pat on the back," they have probably been uncomfortable with that person for other subtle behaviors. Pay attention. Second, suppose you had a man who served in combat working for you and another person had a habit of coming up behind him and clapping loudly just to watch him startle. Would you tell the combat veteran to "get over it" because it's no big deal? Or would you tell the other person to stop the behavior that provokes his startled response?

## I. REVIEW QUESTIONS

When a person has been traumatized, their brain _____

_____ by the event.


People who were traumatized in the past may respond

based on how their brains were _____

during those previous traumatic experiences.


Consider the legal doctrine of the "eggshell skull." Who is

held liable and why?


If someone has suffered significantly, some might shrug it

off but you MUST _____

_____.

When traumatized, our _____ are impaired, and we may _____ the order of events.

If someone is babbling endlessly, not focusing on the questions, or shifting from anger to laughter to crying while narrating the event, they may be _____ _____.

Do everything in your power to help claimants _____ _____ talking to you.

An appropriate, _____ response will help *you* avoid _____.

<u>Do</u> ask how the claimant is feeling and if they _____ _____.

The safer the person feels with you, the more likely the _____ will subside.

## II. REFLECTION QUESTIONS

How does understanding the impact of trauma on the brain help you make sense of what a person is reporting and how they are behaving? In what ways might that understanding help you do your job better?

List five behaviors a traumatized person might display that could affect how you interpret the complaint or report they are bringing to you.

1. _____

2. _____

3. _____

4. _____

5. _____

# ADDITIONAL NOTES:

# CHAPTER 2

## ACCOUNTABLE

The second aspect of an On-TARGET Response is to be accountable. Note that I didn't say be "held" accountable. It might turn out that your organization must be held accountable, but at the initial stages of the inquiry and investigation, it's enough that you just be accountable. That means you take responsibility for investigating the matter fairly and professionally. It means you remain accountable to all involved by answering their questions and addressing their concerns. To be accountable means to handle the situation honorably. If someone tells you they were injured on your property or by someone in your charge, your responsibility is to ensure that you find out what happened, take steps to ensure it doesn't happen again, and do everything in your power to help the injured person.

Accountability is about relationships. It means acknowledging you have a relationship with the person who is injured, as well as a relationship with the person or people alleged to have caused that injury. That may not be a comfortable place to be, but your role is to navigate these relationships in a manner that preserves the integrity of your organization, yourself, and the injured party. That might mean severing the relationship with those who have caused the injury. It should never mean severing the relationship with the injured party except to the extent they want that relationship severed. Even then, you want them to leave feeling as if they've been heard and respected and you've done everything you can to make it right.

When you are accountable, you take ownership of the problem. You make a commitment to do everything in your power to address it. What you don't do is make commitments you can't keep or communicate that you will do something beyond your power. You don't tell someone that you'll see to it that so-and-so is fired. Instead, you tell them that you will investigate, provide them with resources, explain what you can and can't do, and discuss potential outcomes. By clarifying what you can and cannot do, you will avoid setting expectations you can't fulfill. They may be disappointed you can't do more, but they won't feel you've let them down by making false promises. Being accountable means you won't blame others, you won't delegate responsibility, and you won't play favorites. And it means that you hold those you supervise accountable. That's not just good ethics. That's leadership.

## TAKEAWAYS

- Being accountable is not the same as being held accountable.
- You may ultimately be held accountable, but focus on being accountable to your organization and to those affected by your organization and its agents.
- Accountability is about maintaining relationships, both your relationship to your organization and to those it serves.

- Being accountable means being responsible—by finding out what happened, taking steps to ensure it does not happen again, and doing everything in your power to help the injured person.
- Being accountable means holding others accountable, as well. That's not the same as shifting blame or delegating responsibility. It means you have a professional standard that accepts responsibility for the good and the bad and you expect everyone you supervise to do the same.
- It's not enough to say you're accountable. You need to show it. Demonstrate your sense of accountability by following up. Meet with the person periodically to ensure that the process is moving along and they understand it, determine whether there's anything more you can do, and identify problems as they arise.

## FAQS

Q. *I'm not responsible for something I had no control over. Why am I responsible for something someone else did?*

A. You are responsible for doing your job and, depending on your role, you will have different responsibilities when it comes to addressing a problem someone's brought to you. You no doubt have a responsibility to your organization. Part of that responsibility is finding out what happened, who was involved, when and where it happened, and assessing any potential liability your organization may have. To do so, you owe it to yourself, your organization, and anyone who comes to you for help to be true to your values and responsible for handling the matter with integrity and fairness.

**Q. *I'm afraid I'm putting my organization at risk if I express any accountability or responsibility for the incident. How can I ensure that taking responsibility for something doesn't imply liability?***

A. Being accountable does not mean admitting you're at fault. If anything, being accountable can minimize litigation because you are addressing the problem right from the onset. It means doing everything you can to take ownership of the problem. When you do that, the person feels heard.

**Q. *If being accountable means I don't delegate responsibility, how do I make sure each party does their job?***

A. Whatever your role, you are accountable for upholding your end of the deal. You are responsible for the people you supervise and the units or departments you are charged with. You must ensure that the process is followed. The investigators investigate, HR handles employment matters, resources are communicated and the person can access them, and risk management and the legal department are alerted. But you don't say that what your employees, clients, students, or other stakeholders do is not your responsibility. You don't say you'll have someone else handle the matter (unless there is a conflict of interest). You find out what happened. You understand the process for reporting and investigating these matters, and you communicate with other units to ensure that the process is followed and understood by all, especially the person making the claim.

## I. REVIEW QUESTIONS

To be accountable means to handle the _____

_____.

When you are accountable, you take _____

of the problem.

Being accountable means you won't _____

others, you won't delegate responsibility, and you won't

_____.

Accountability is about _____

—both your relationship to your organization and _____

_____.

Demonstrate your _____

by following up.

Being accountable can minimize litigation because you are

_____ right from

the onset.

## II. REFLECTION QUESTIONS

What are your values as a professional? List five values you consider essential to your job.

1. _____

2. _____

3. _____

4. _____

5. _____

Now reflect on how you can maintain these values when faced with a problematic report. Imagine someone comes to you reporting an injury or loss they've suffered and they view your organization as responsible in some way. You are uncertain about the report and want to safeguard your organization's reputation and limit their liability. How can you remain accountable to both your organization and the person making the report in a manner that remains true to these values?

What are your professional responsibilities when a complaint is brought to your attention?

**Who do you need to communicate with?**

**What part of the process do you own?**

**What commitment can you make to the person bringing a complaint to you?**

**ADDITIONAL NOTES:**

# CHAPTER 3
## RESPECTFUL & RESPONSIVE

t's easy to feel defensive and look for holes in any claimant's story, especially if traumatized behavior is influencing your perceptions of their credibility. Be careful. If you find yourself either interrogating or, on the other extreme, being dismissive of their concerns, the person will feel disrespected and any trauma they are suffering will ensure a heightened sensitivity to feeling disrespected and disbelieved.

Don't allow the process to become adversarial. Show them respect. Acknowledge their feelings, don't talk down to them, and address them with humility. If you do not already know them by their first name, don't address them by their first name without asking. Assume that what they are telling you is true and continue to do so unless proven otherwise. Rarely will someone in any organizational setting make up an injury that hasn't happened. Yes, there will be the occasional con artist who thinks they can profit from some fabricated injury or the malingerer who exaggerates their injuries for attention or profit, but they are the exceptions, not the rule. The rule is that when someone comes to you with a report of injury or loss, they are telling you something you need to know, and they need your help. Start there.

In addition to being respectful, you must be responsive. Being responsive is a step beyond being accountable. To be responsive means you acknowledge their injuries. It means you tell them what you can do, what you will do, and then you do it. If you can call for an investigation, do so. If you can intervene to prevent the incident from happening again, do so. If you can take steps to protect this person and others from the same future injury, do so. If you can meet with colleagues or other relevant parties to ensure that the process is handled appropriately, do so. And just like being accountable, follow up. Connect with them again to see how they are doing and find out what more they need. If you can meet those needs, do so. If someone else can meet those needs, have them do so. In other words, take action to help in any way you can while preventing that same problem from reoccurring.

## TAKEAWAYS

- Even if you're suspicious about a complaint, show respect. You'll get more cooperation and are more likely to get the truth.
- Keep your own emotions in check. Most people who report an injury or loss are telling the truth. Those who are not truthful are the exception, not the rule.
- Someone who has been traumatized by an injury or loss is suffering. Respect their pain and do not exacerbate it.
- It's not enough to just listen respectfully. You must also be responsive. Take action to address their needs,

provide them with resources, facilitate the reporting process, and communicate with other relevant parties.

## FAQS

**Q. *How do I show respect for someone I know who has been a problem from day one?***

A. Being problematic in the past does not equate to lying or exaggerating now. Presume the person is telling you the truth and respect that, regardless of your biases, they are in pain. Or consider the ramifications: if you don't do everything you can to address the problem, the problem won't go away, may reoccur, and someone else may suffer from the same injury or loss.

**Q. *How can you expect me to respect someone I know is racist/sexist/homophobic/ultra-liberal/ultra-conservative? I can take their report and send it up the pipeline, but don't tell me to respect them. I won't.***

A. That's a statement that reflects an unwillingness to be responsive and a disregard for what happened because it's focused more on how YOU feel rather than the issue being reported. Focus on the humanity of the person before you. Regardless of your feelings for them personally or politically, respond to their pain. Someone is hurting and they need your help. Disrespect and mistreatment will likely make the problem worse and, chances are, you'll be dealing with them much more often and in an adversarial manner.

**Q. *How am I supposed to be responsive when my job is to just take the report and send it up the pipeline?***

A. You can also point them to resources, explain the process to them, follow up to ensure that the problem is being addressed, and check in with them to see how they are doing. If you show you care and will help in any way you can, they will feel heard, helped, and hopeful. They are also less likely to file a lawsuit if they feel you've been respectful and responsive.

## I. REVIEW QUESTIONS

Don't allow the process to become _____.

Rarely will someone in any organizational setting make up an injury that hasn't _____.

There will be the occasional con artist who thinks they can profit from some _____ injury, but they are the _____, not the rule.

In addition to being respectful, you must _____ _____.

If you don't do everything you can to address the problem, the problem won't _____.

Presume the person is telling you _____ and respect that, regardless of your biases, _____ _____.

## II. REFLECTION QUESTIONS

**What are some of the characteristics of people whom you don't respect?**

Imagine someone with these qualities coming to you with a report of injury or loss. How might you set aside your own emotions and help them? What will it take for you to treat and assist them just as you would someone you admire?

Given your professional responsibilities and role, identify five things you could do to help someone who comes to you with a report of injury or loss.

1. _____

2. _____

3. _____

4. _____

5. _____

Imagine you've been injured by someone's acts, or failure to act, and you've reported your injuries to someone responsible for looking into such matters. Imagine you feel angry and frightened about how people will perceive you when you make the report, and you haven't been sleeping well. How would you want to be treated? Describe what such an encounter would look like. What would they say to you and how would they respond to your report? If they had doubts about your report or the cause of the injury, how would you want them to express those concerns?

## ADDITIONAL NOTES:

# CHAPTER 4

## GENUINE

Thus far you've been hearing that you need to show respect to people you might not personally respect, treat every report as credible even if you have concerns about its credibility, and help people who may pose a litigation risk to your organization. So, how do you do all that while appearing genuine? Isn't that a contradiction?

It's not if you focus on the humanity of every person you deal with. We live in such a polarized world that it's easy to dismiss people we disagree with, reduce people to stereotypical images based on their views or lifestyle, and become cynical about the motivations of anyone we perceive as a tattletale, at best, or scammer, at worst. But none of these attitudes will help you do a better job. The more you respond based on prejudices, assumptions, and "hunches" or "gut feelings," the more likely the claimant will not trust you, will not be open with you, and will do everything they can to get help elsewhere—whether that's through litigation, going to the press and/or social media, or going over your head and telling your supervisors you've made the problem worse.

To avoid such an outcome, be genuine. Talk from the heart as if someone you care for is telling you what happened. Don't make false promises, provide false assurances, or talk to them like you're reading from a book of rules. No one likes the officious administrator who does nothing more than recite the rules. Someone who has been traumatized needs human interaction. That doesn't mean reaching out and hugging them. Indeed, you should never touch them or encroach on their personal space. It doesn't mean asking probing, personal questions. It does mean being empathetic. It does mean asking about their support system if relevant. And it does mean speaking from the heart.

## TAKEAWAYS

- Being genuine means speaking to the humanity of the person before you—from your own humanity.
- Being genuine means being empathetic, but not providing false promises or assurances of any outcome.
- Being genuine means not just telling someone you'll do something; it means doing it. By following through and establishing trust early on, you'll set the stage for a constructive outcome.
- Be genuine, but don't invade someone's personal space or ask questions that are not your business. Asking if they have a support network is one thing. Asking if they are married, if they have any friends, and other specifics is not appropriate.

## FAQS

Q. *How am I supposed to be genuine while pretending I respect a person that I don't respect?*

A. When focusing on the claimant's humanity, you shouldn't have to fake anything. Who they are isn't your concern. What happened to them is. Focus on that and understand that, regardless of what you think of them personally, hurt is hurt. Keep your focus on resolving that hurt as much as possible and finding out what happened.

**Q. *My supervisor told me to make this problem go away. Being "genuine" would mean telling them they don't stand a chance.***

A. Being genuine means speaking from the heart, taking their report, offering empathy, explaining the process, and pointing them to resources. The more you do so, the more likely the problem will "go away" once the person feels heard, respected, and responded to. The more you treat them otherwise, the more likely the problem will get bigger. Don't tell them they don't stand a chance. Tell them how the process works.

## I. REVIEW QUESTIONS

Treat every report as _____ even if you have concerns about its credibility.

The more you respond based on prejudices, assumptions, and "hunches" or "gut feelings," the more likely the claimant will not _____.

Talk from the heart as if _____ _____ is telling you what happened.

Don't just recite the rules. Someone who has been traumatized needs_____.

Being _____ means being empathetic.

By _____ trust early on, you'll set the stage for a constructive outcome.

Being genuine means speaking _____, offering empathy, and pointing them to resources.

## II. REFLECTION QUESTIONS

How do you genuinely feel when someone reports a problem to you? Does it depend on the person who makes the report? Do you feel annoyed by the extra work it will create? Do you fear you'll cross your superiors if you don't make the problem "go away"? Write out how you genuinely feel when someone comes to you with a problem.

Do you believe most people are telling the truth when they report an injury or loss, that most people are lying, or that some lie, and some tell the truth? Think through your assumptions about these reports. If you think some tell the truth and some lie, how can you tell the difference? What kinds of people are more apt to lie and who is more likely to be telling the truth in your view?

What qualities do you bring to the table that will help you handle these reports? List the qualities you feel you already possess and how you demonstrate them in your work.

Quality:

How it's demonstrated:

Quality:

How it's demonstrated:

**Quality:**


**How it's demonstrated:**


**Quality:**


**How it's demonstrated:**

# ADDITIONAL NOTES:

# CHAPTER 5

## EMPOWERING

Perhaps the idea of empowering a claimant is troubling if you consider that they could sue or create negative press, and cause harm to your organization. So, why should you?

Empowering someone who has been traumatized by an injury or loss is not about strengthening their case against you. Empowerment is about giving people *some* control over the process, which in turn makes it less likely they will sue you or go to the press.

Whenever someone has suffered a traumatic injury or loss, they feel helpless. Something has happened beyond their control and they cannot undo it. That sense of powerlessness can lead people to make threats, take legal action, or go to the press—anything that gives them a sense of control. They may also become angry, enraged even, by any sense of injustice, disrespect, slight, or further injury. Anger is an emotion that gives some people a sense of power. Displaying other emotions might leave them feeling more powerless, but anger is associated with strength. When you empower the claimant, you reduce their need to seek power elsewhere. So, what does "empower them" mean and how do you do it? Begin with helping them identify and take control over different elements of the process. Present them with options. They may choose to file a formal report, request an investigation, or grant permission for a representative to speak with someone involved in the matter, such as a witness or the person(s) accused, if any. Other options might involve relocating them; reassigning them to someone new such as a new advisor to a student or a new doctor to a patient; or any other choices they can make that might address the problem. The more you can present people with choices without omitting important information such as costs or losses associated with that choice, the more they will feel empowered. The more they feel empowered, the less likely they'll try to exert power over you.

Simple questions like, "Is it alright with you if I . . ." or "What can I do to help you?" or "What can we do to make it right?" can go a long way. Keep in mind the importance of being genuine. Don't present choices they don't really have or imply that they have control over an element of the process that is entirely beyond their control. To the extent the process has to be followed in a specific manner, say so. But to the extent there are choices to be made, let the person know about these choices. Ask them about witnesses and contact their witnesses. Don't declare that you'll decide who to contact, and then only contact witnesses who will support one side of a dispute. If a claimant offers evidence, don't refuse to review it. The more a claimant feels involved in how the process unfolds, the less victimized they will feel by the process itself. It's when the process re-victimizes someone who has already been traumatized that the experience becomes a nightmare for all, and the damage escalates.

## TAKEAWAYS

- Empowering someone means helping them feel they have some control over what is happening.
- When people feel they have some control, they're less likely to act out of control—which helps you do your job.
- By helping claimants to identify areas where they have some control over the process, you help calm them and facilitate a trusting relationship.

## FAQS

**Q. We can't just let these people control the process. We have a specific way we handle these matters and it's not up to someone else to determine how we do it. Why should we give up control?**

A. First, helping a claimant find some control over certain elements of the process is not putting them in control of the whole thing. You're presenting them with choices wherever you can without disrupting important protocols. Second, by empowering someone who feels their injury or loss has robbed them unjustly and at no fault of their own, you are not giving up control. You are showing them that they do still have power and a voice concerning their own life and how things proceed from there.

**Q. What about our options? Don't we have a say in whether we investigate something and how we investigate it?**

A. Depending on the nature of the report, you may be required by law to investigate. Moreover, failure to investigate a report of injury, assault, harm, or other grievous loss can increase your liability and cost your organization more money. As for how you investigate, what matters is that you conduct a thorough and fair investigation. That means you consider all the evidence and witnesses that all parties present to you. You may only want to take a quick glance at the problem and conclude it's not a problem, but if you do so, the problem won't go away—it will get bigger.

## I. REVIEW QUESTIONS

Empowerment is about giving people _____ control over the process.

A sense of _____ can lead people to make threats.

The more you can present people _____ without _____ important information, the more they will feel empowered.

If a claimant offers evidence, don't_____ to _____ it.

You may only want to take a _____ at the problem and conclude it's not a problem, but if you do so, the problem won't go away—it will

_____.

## II. REFLECTION QUESTIONS

When someone comes to you with a grievance or report of injury or loss, what are some choices they can make about next steps?

What are some of your own fears about sharing control with others? In what ways might sharing control with others leave you feeling more in control and/or empower *you* and help make your job easier?

## ADDITIONAL NOTES:

# CHAPTER 6

## TRANSPARENT

Finally, an On-TARGET Response means being transparent. All too often investigations are conducted and reports generated without the central player ever knowing about it. After the injury, harm, or loss occurs, the claimant may wait months, even years, for findings only to be told the matter was reviewed and closed long ago. They may be told "investigations are ongoing," but they are not to know anything about what is happening until the final report is submitted. While there may indeed be sound legal justification for not sharing the details of an investigation, keeping them periodically informed and answering their questions with as much information as possible minimizes their stress, which reduces their desire to pursue legal action.

Some of the areas where you can be transparent include explaining the process, telling them who you've spoken with, providing them with copies of all findings and reports that have been generated, and answering their questions as clearly and specifically as possible. Withholding documents they request and to which they have a legal right will not help you. It will demonstrate a willful lack of cooperation. They may not have a right to internal communications, but if there is something they do have a legal right to and they request it, comply with the request in a respectful and timely manner. Avoid secret meetings, secret investigations, and other opaque measures that assure an adversarial experience for all. Discretion is one thing, concealing the steps you are taking is another. Be transparent and there should be no surprises.

## TAKEAWAYS

- Being transparent means explaining the process, giving updates, answering questions, and providing reports as they are generated.
- Opaque proceedings like secret investigations can cause undue frustration that could lead someone to file lawsuits, open records requests, or even going to the press to find out what is happening.
- A failure to be transparent is disempowering and an unnecessary source of stress that can further intensify a person's trauma, which has the potential to increase any damage award.
- Avoid secrecy. That does not mean you can't have discretion and respect confidential information, but secret meetings and investigations always come to light eventually. The more you avoid secrecy, the less stressful the experience is for all.

## FAQS

*Q. I don't have time to tell someone every time I do something. At what point does this "transparency" end so I can do my job?*

A. No one expects you to update claimants every step of the way, but answer their questions. If you initiate an investigation, let them know about it. If there is an important meeting held about the matter that involves a number of different people, tell them about it in advance, if possible, rather than having them hear about it through the rumor mill. If you write a report, provide them with a copy.

**Q.** *How do I know if I can share information with them? Isn't some of it confidential?*

A. Yes, some information is confidential. There are different rules for different types of information. Your legal counsel and risk management team can answer these questions for you, but you should share findings and reports. Disclose investigations that are conducted. Generally, you'll be aware of any efforts to suppress information. When that happens, make the case for not suppressing anything. It all comes out in the discovery process. If you don't want it to get that far, reveal the information early on and address it.

## I. REVIEW QUESTIONS

Keeping claimants periodically informed and answering their questions minimizes their stress, which reduces their

_____.

Some of the areas where you can be transparent include:

explaining _____

telling them _____

providing _____

answering _____

Avoid secret investigations, and other opaque measures that assure an _____ experience for all.

A failure to be transparent is _____ and an unnecessary source of stress.

No one expects you to update claimants every step of the way, but _____.

## II. REFLECTION QUESTIONS

Have you ever been told by a supervisor to keep something secret, leaving you feeling uncomfortable or deceitful? What happened and how did you feel?

If a supervisor instructed you to withhold important information to a party who has brought a report of injury or loss to you, but you feel doing so is unethical or might breach the trust you've been trying to establish with them, how might you argue for being more transparent?

Imagine you are explaining the process to someone who has been injured or harmed. You come to the point where you must inform them of what you can and cannot share. What are some types of information you cannot share with them?

What are some types of information you can share with them?

## ADDITIONAL NOTES:

# CONCLUSION

Understanding the impact of trauma on anyone who has suffered an injury or loss or been harmed in any way can go far in protecting your organization from unnecessary lawsuits. And if there is a lawsuit, the more you can demonstrate that you've treated the plaintiff fairly and humanely, the better the outcome for your organization. In contrast, if you treat a traumatized plaintiff badly, withhold information, and fail to clarify their options and the process they must follow, then you will likely expose your organization to higher damages.

By employing an On-TARGET Response, you can stay focused on how to safeguard your organization while minimizing the stress for everyone involved. An On-TARGET Response means understanding what Trauma does to the brain and how it affects behavior, cognition, communication, and memory. It means being Accountable and taking responsibility for helping the person who has come to you for help. It means being Respectful and Responsive to anyone who comes to you for help—regardless of how you might feel about them personally. It means being Genuine and not coming across like you're giving them a sales pitch or deceiving them with slick promises you won't keep. It means Empowering them to make choices— to know what choices they can make, to understand where they do have some control over what happens, and to encourage them to take that control—so that the process doesn't spiral. And finally, an On-TARGET Response means being Transparent —not concealing important information, avoiding their calls, or holding secret investigations and meetings you don't want them to find out about. It means letting them know what's going on throughout the process.

It's all too easy to adopt a defensive position when someone comes to you with a complaint, especially if it's a complaint that could land your organization in court facing a potential jury award. These situations can cost people their careers as political allegiances are tested, and any mistakes can make the problem worse. But as a plaintiff attorney, I can assure you that anyone who has been traumatized by an injury or loss will feel re-traumatized if they are treated badly and their determination to get justice will be even greater. Conversely, treating them humanely, acknowledging their trauma, clarifying the process, and helping them understand the choices they have along the way will go far in reducing the stress for everyone—and often prevents a lawsuit.

Don't make a person bringing the complaint *a* target by re-traumatizing them during the process. And don't make your organization *the* target of a lawyer who will fight tirelessly to ensure the highest reward for their client. By implementing an On-TARGET Response from the onset, you'll probably never find yourself on the witness stand having to justify why you didn't treat the plaintiff fairly when you were asked to help.

# ADDITIONAL NOTES:

**IF YOU'RE A FAN OF *WIN WIN*, WILL YOU HELP SPREAD THE WORD?**

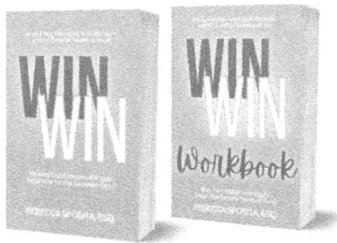

There are several ways you can let others know about *WIN WIN*…

- Post a 5-Star review on Amazon.
- Write about *WIN WIN* on your social media accounts.
- If you podcast or blog, consider referencing *WIN WIN*, or publish an excerpt with a link back to the website: www.rebeccasposita.com.
- Recommend *WIN WIN* to friends. Word of mouth is still the most effective form of advertising.
- Purchase additional copies to distribute or sell to clients, prospects, team members, donors, brokers, dealers, associates, co-workers, family, and friends.

www.ingramcontent.com/pod-product-compliance
Lightning Source LLC
Chambersburg PA
CBHW071441210326
41597CB00020B/3902